The Self Life and the Christ Life

A. B. Simpson

The Self Life and the Christ Life

ISBN: 978-1-61895-381-0

Contents

Chapter 1   Not I but Christ 1

Chapter 2   Resurrected not Raised 16

Chapter 3   Saul, or Self Life Leading to

Destruction 30

Chapter 4   Agag, or the Subtleties of the Self Life. 43

Chapter 5   Jonah, or the Shadow of Self 56

Chapter 1

NOT I BUT CHRIST

"If any man will come after me, let him deny himself, and take up his cross, and follow me." (Mat. 16: 24). "I am crucified with Christ: nevertheless I live; yet not I, but Christ." (Gal. 2: 20).

HERE lies the great difference between the world's gospel and the Lord's Gospel. The world says, when it bids you good-bye, "Take care of yourself." The Lord says, "Let yourself go, and take care of others and the glory of your God." The world says, "Have a good time, look out for Number One." But the world gets left in the end, and the last comes in first. The man that lets go gets all, and the man who holds fast loses what he has, and the Lord's words come true – "Whosoever will save his life shall lose it: and whosoever will lose his life for my sake shall find it."

So the law of sacrifice is the greatest law in earth and heaven. The law of sacrifice is God's great law. It is written in earth and every department of nature. We tread on the skeletons of ten thousand millions of generations that have lived and died that we might

1

live. The very heart of the earth itself is the wreck of ages and the buried life of former generations. All nature dies and lives again, and each new development is a higher and larger life built on the wrecks of the former. A corn of wheat must fall into the ground and die, or else be a shrivelled-up seed, but as it dies it lives and multiplies, and grows into the beautiful spring, the golden autumn and the multiplied sheaves. And so it is in the deeper life of the higher world, as you rise from the natural to the spiritual. Everything that is selfish is limited by its selfishness. The river that ceases to run becomes a stagnant pool, but as it flows it grows fresher, richer, fuller.

If you turn your natural eye upon yourself, you cannot see anything. It is as you look out that the vision of the world bursts upon you. The very law of the natural life is love for others, caring for others by giving away and letting go. It is death and self-destruction to be selfish.

The law of sacrifice is the law of God. God who lived in supreme self-sufficiency as the Father, Son and Holy Ghost gave Himself. God's glory was in giving Himself, and so He gave Himself in the creation, in the beauty of the universe, so formed that every possible sort of happiness could come according to its natural law. And then God gave Himself in Jesus Christ. "God so loved the world that he gave." He gave His best, gave His all, gave His only begotten Son. The law of God is sacrifice. He loved until he gave ALL.

Then it is the law of Christ Himself. He came through God's sacrifice, and He came to sacrifice. He laid His honors down, left the society of heaven for a generation, and lived with creatures farther beneath Him than the grovelling earth worm is beneath man. He made Himself one of them, and became a brother of this fallen race. He was always yielding and letting go, always holding back His power and not using it. He was always being subject to the will of the men beneath Him, until at last they nailed Him to the cross. His whole life was a continual refusing of Himself, carrying their burdens and sharing their sorrows. And so love and sacrifice is the law of Christ. "Bear ye one another's burdens, and so fulfill the law of Christ." The law of Christ is the bearing of others' burdens, the sharing of others' griefs, sacrificing yourself for another.

It is the law of Christianity. It is the law of the saint. It is the only way to be saved. From the beginning it has always been so. It was so on Mt. Moriah where Abraham, the father of the faithful, gave up his only child, the child of promise. It reached its climax on Mt. Calvary. All along, the way was marked by blood and sacrifice. Not only did Abraham give up his Isaac but

Isaac gave up his life and all through his life he laid himself down for others. We know how Jacob served for his wife, and then did not get the one of his choice. His was a suffering life, a passive life, a patient life. And so Joseph died to his circumstances. Because he was to rise so high, he must go down as low; down not only into banishment but into shameful imprisonment and almost into death. When Joseph was out of sight and all God's promises concerning him seemed lost, and his prospects seemed hopeless, then God picked him up and set him on the world's throne.

Moses had to be a fugitive. Moses had to try and then fail and for forty years God had to teach him and train him, and when at last Moses was out of sight, He gave him his desire. At the very last moment Moses had to let go the prospect of entering the Promised Land. He died outside the gates of Canaan, sacrificed his most cherished hope and waited till the years should roll and Jesus Himself should bring him in to stand with Him on the Mount of Transfiguration and say, "Now, Moses, you have the thing you let go, the thing you lost and died to, and now you have a better resurrection." And so it was all through the past. Saul would not give up himself, would not destroy Agag and Amalek, types of the flesh. So Saul, head and shoulders above the people, all that a man could be, went down into the darkness, sank into obscurity and shame and perhaps perdition. And Jonah, the man whom God honored to deliver His own people and lead His kingdom into victory and mighty power in the days of Jeroboam II, the man whom God honored to be the first foreign missionary, the man whom God had picked up and sent to Assyria, and said, Go and preach to Nineveh, go bring the world to know and honor me; was so greatly blessed that in that city the mightiest revival the world ever saw was consummated. And yet Jonah got angry because He did not kill all the people in Nineveh, and so compromised Jonah's reputation. Jonah had said that the people would die in forty days and before the forty days were up the people repented of their sins and God repented of what He said and forgave them, and Jonah said, "Where am I in this transaction? I will never be believed again. Why did you not destroy Nineveh and save my reputation?" And because Jonah could not let his own glory go, God had to dishonor him and leave him under the withered gourd, a sort of scare-crow to show to all generations how contemptible it is to seek one's own glory. I think there is no more shocking and ridiculous spectacle than that poor old prophet sitting under his withered gourd scolding God and begging to die just because he felt God had dishonored him in fulfilling his mission in the repentance of the whole nation. And God just let him stand there as a spectacle of the shame and dishonor of selfishness.

We need not trace through the New Testament the story of Simon Peter. The Master's last message to him when He restored him was: "When thou wast young, thou girdedst thyself, and walkedst whither thou wouldest: but when thou shalt be old, thou shall stretch forth thy hands, and another shall gird thee, and carry thee whither thou wouldest not. This spake he, signifying by what death he should glorify God." And Jesus sent him to a life of crucifixion to be yielded, submissive, surrendered and led about by others against his natural choice till at last he should be crucified with downward head upon his Master's cross.

The world says, look out for yourself; but Jesus says, "Not I, but Christ." Not only your old self but the new man with all his strength and self-confidence, too, must die. Not only Ishmael must go out and be an outcast, but Isaac must be yielded and not hold up his head again.

It is so easy to talk about this. The longer I live, the longer I know myself and friends, the more thoroughly I am satisfied that this is the great secret of failure in our Christian life. We come a little way with Jesus but we stop at Gethsemane and Calvary. They followed

Him in His ministry in Galilee. The Sermon on the Mount was splendid morality. They loved the feeding of the thousands, and said, What a blessed King He would make! They would not have to work as they used to. But when He stands and talks about Calvary and speaks of the cross for them as well as for Him, and how they must go with Him and go with Him all the way, they say, "This is a hard saying; who can bear it?"

And a few days after you could count them on your fingers. They said we do not understand Him; we thought He would be a king. They were not willing to go to the cross.

I am sure this is where multitudes have stopped short. They have said yes to self and no to God, instead of saying no to self and yes to God. Oh! it is so much easier to talk than to live! There is no use to talk about it unless the Holy Ghost shall bring it home to us. A writer has recently said that there are three baptisms to be baptized with. First, the baptism of repentance, then we turned from sin to God. Second, the baptism of the Holy Ghost, when we receive the Holy Spirit to live in us. Third, the baptism into death, after the Holy Spirit comes in. While he, perhaps, has no Scriptural authority for this precise distinction, there is no doubt that there are these three steps to take. After you receive the baptism of the Holy Ghost, after God comes to live in you, after the Holy Spirit makes your heart His home, then it is that you have to go with Christ into His own dying, and so He says, "If any man will come after me, let him deny himself, and take up his cross daily, and follow me." And so He said about Himself, "I have a baptism to be baptized with; and how am I straitened till it be accomplished!" I have a burial to be buried with. He was going out into deeper dying every day, and His heart was all pent up with it, until He went down into Gethsemane, down to Joseph's tomb, and down into Hades, and He passed through the regions of the dead and opened first the gates of heaven. That is what Jesus saw before Him after He was baptized on the banks of Jordan.

Oh! beloved, who have received the baptism of the Holy Ghost, it is you who have to go down into His death. Now, I know that in a sense we take all that by faith when we consecrate ourselves to Christ, and we count it all real and God counts it all real; but, my dear friends, you have to go through it step by step. I know God treats us as though it was accomplished, as though we were sitting yonder on the throne. But we must go through the narrow passage and the secret places of the stairs. There must be no fooling here. You may count it all done; but step by step it must be written on the records of your heart.

Now, my friends, what does all this mean? It is dying to self-will. After you consecrate yourself to God, then comes the tug of war, and tomorrow morning you will have the most awful battle of your life. Just because you have given up your will, the devil wants you to take it back. Do not think it will be an Elysian field; no, it will be a battlefield; battles with the dragon and the fiery darts. The devil will try to show you how unreasonable it is, how right it is that you should stand and have your will. It will be life or death perhaps for a week or for a month. Jesus went into the wilderness for forty days, and the devil tried to have Him have His own will, but He stood the test. He let His own will go, "I came . . . not to do mine own will, but the will of him that sent me."

God could make Him a leader because He had been led. No man can govern until he has been governed. Joseph could not have been where he was in Egypt unless he had been sat upon by the people and then he sat there a broken man and a lowly, humble spirit. His brothers came down to see him. The world would have said, Make them feel how mean they were and how wicked. God said, No, help them to forget it; and so Joseph said, Don't be angry or grieved with yourselves, God meant it "for good." If Joseph had not been humbled, he would have been no good as Egypt's ruler. No man can lead until he has been led. David had to have nine years of training, and it might have been better for him to have had nine more, then he would not have abused so shamefully his power when he got to the throne. Daniel in Babylon had to be disciplined by suffering before he could sit as Premier with Cyrus and Nebuchadnezzar. If God is going to make anything of you, let all your will go into His hands. You will find a good many tests after the first surrender, but these are just opportunities for allowing the work to be done.

Then comes self-indulgence, doing a thing because you like to do it. No man has a right to do a thing for the pleasure it affords, because he enjoys or likes it. I have no right to take my dinner just because I like it. This makes me a beast. I do it because it nourishes me. Doing things because they please yourself, seeking your own interest, is wrong. "Seek ye first the kingdom of God, and his righteousness." We have no Divine warrant to seek ourselves in anything. Seek God, and God will seek your good. Take care of the things of God, because He will take care of you. Look not any man on your own things, but on the things of others.

Again, there is self-complacency, dwelling on the work that you have done. How easy after performing some service or gaining some victory to think, "How good." How quickly this runs into vain glory! How many are more interested in what people think and say of them than what they are themselves.

In the work of God there is nothing we need to so guard against as vanity. That was Jonah's curse. The seraphim covered their faces with their wings, they covered their feet with their wings. They covered their faces because they did not want to see their beauty, and their feet because they did not want to see their service, nor have anyone else see them. They used only two to fly. Take care how you put temptation in another's way. It is all right to encourage workers with a "God bless you." But don't praise. God does not say, How beautiful, how eloquent, how lovely, how splendid! That is putting on a human head the crown that belongs to Jesus. I want the Holy Ghost to enable me simply to do you good, but I do not want power to bring me the honor of the world. If I had it, I should feel it the greatest peril of my life. We have no more right to take Christ's honors here than we have to sit on Jesus' throne and let angels worship us. We have to be so careful when God uses us to bless human souls. There is a sweetness which is not of God. God save us from all these snares woven by the tempter.

Philip as soon as he had led the eunuch to Jesus got out of the eunuch's way. Beloved, there are subtle spells that come between man and man, and between woman and woman, and between man and woman. They seem sweet and right, but you need much of the Holy Ghost to keep your spirit pure. I am not talking here of sinful love. Surely, it is not needful to speak of that. I am thinking of a far more subtle and refined and spotless spell, which is more dishonoring to God and more dangerous to you, because it is so pure. God keep us from every service, and every friendship, and every thought that is not in the Holy Ghost and not to the honor of Jesus alone.

Then there is self-confidence, that which feels its strength, spiritual or mental self-righteousness, power to be good or do good. God has to lead us to lay all that aside and realize our utter nothingness.

Time will not permit me to speak of the self life of sensitiveness, that fine susceptibility of your feelings to be wounded, and of selfish affection, wanting people to love you because you like to be loved. Divine love loves that it may bless and do good. You ought to love not because it pleases you, but because it blesses them. Paul could say, "And I will very gladly spend and be spent for you; though the more abundantly I love you, the less I be loved." He does not say, I will help you as long as you love me. No; I gladly spend my last drop of blood to bless you at any cost even when I know you don't appreciate me the least bit. That is what is the matter with you. People hurt you, they don't appreciate you. Well, spend and be spent all the more when you are the less loved.

Time would fail to tell of selfish desires, covetousness, selfish motives, selfish possessions, our property our own, our children our own, and they give us loads of trouble, and care, and worry, just because we insist on owning them.

There are selfish sorrows. I know of nothing more selfish than the tears we shed for our own sorrows. When God saw Israel weeping, He was angry and said, "You have polluted my altar with your tears." You are weeping because you have not better bread. You are weeping because something else is dearer to you than Christ. You are weeping because you are not altogether pleased or gratified.

Even our sacrifices and self-denials may be selfish. Yes, our sanctification may be selfish. A sarcastic friend of mine used to say when he heard people testify about their sinlessness, "Poor old soul, she committed the biggest sin of her life for she told the biggest lie." Self can get up and pray, and sit down and say, "What a lovely prayer!" Self can preach a sermon and save souls and go home, pat itself on the back and say, or let the devil say through him, "You did splendidly; what a useful man you are!" Self can be burned to death and be proud of its fortitude. Yes, we can have religious selfishness as well as carnal selfishness.

-How can we get rid of this? Well, I think above everything else we must see the reality of the thing, we must see the danger of the thing, we must see that it is our sin. We must look at it frankly and choose that it shall go. The worst of it is that it deceives us so. It says, "How that fits somebody else, not me." Many of you are shedding it on others and not taking it home. God means you. Pass sentence of death upon it or else it will pass sentence on you. You may keep it as long as you like. It is like the lovely little serpent with little spots on it like Jewels. Ah – at the last – how it stings!

May God show us everything in us that will not stand the searching flames. Above everything don't let us have a bigger Gospel than we have a life. Having passed sentence of death upon ourselves then take Jesus Christ and the Holy Spirit to do the work. Don't try to fight it.

Then when the test comes and God leads you out to meet the test, be true, BE TRUE. The test will come in that very line after you have taken the victory, and when the battle comes, forget yourself; don't defend yourself but say, Lord, keep me. Perhaps someone will try to provoke you. Perhaps someone will try to praise you. Just say, Yes, the Lord let you come to see if I wanted to be appreciated. The Holy Spirit is able to take everything we dare to give and gives everything we dare to take. "He is able to keep you from falling and to present you faultless." What a blessed exchange it will be! Take the cross and we shall some day wear the crown, sit upon the throne, and all that He is we shall be, and all that He has we shall share.

Chapter 2

RESURRECTED NOT RAISE

THERE is a great difference between risen and resurrected. One may rise from one level to another; but when one is resurrected he is brought from nothing into existence, from death to life, and the transition is simply infinite. A true Christian is not raised, but resurrected. The great objection to all the teachings of mere natural religion and human ethics is that we are taught to rise to higher planes. The glory of the Gospel is that it does not teach us to rise, but shows our inability to do anything good of ourselves, and lays us at once in the grave in utter helplessness and nothingness, and then raises us up into new life, born entirely from above and sustained alone from heavenly sources.

The Christian life is not self-improving, but it is wholly supernatural and Divine. Now, the resurrection cannot come until there has been the death. This is presupposed, and just as real as the death has been, will be the measure of the resurrection life and power. Let us not fear, therefore, to die and to die to all that we would leave behind us and detach ourselves from, nay, to die to ourselves and really cease to be. We lose nothing by letting go and we cannot enter in 'till we come out. If we be dead with Him, we shall also live with Him.

But the passage Col. 3: 1 expresses the fact that we have already died and risen, and that we are now to take the attitude of those for whom this is an accomplished fact. Paul does not tell them here to die with Christ and rise with Him, but rather he calls upon Christians to take their places as having died and risen with Christ and to live accordingly. He tells them later in verse 3, "For ye are dead, and your life is hid with Christ in God."

In the sixth chapter of Romans this thought is much more fully worked out. "So many of us as were baptized into Jesus Christ," the Apostle says, "were baptized into his death. Therefore we are buried with him by baptism into death: that like as Christ was raised up from the dead by the glory of the Father, even so we also should walk in newness of life." To emphasize more forcibly the finality of this fact, he says, "Knowing that Christ being raised from the dead dieth no more; death hath no more dominion over him. For in that he died, he died unto sin once: but in that he liveth, he liveth unto God." Therefore, and in like

17

manner, the Apostle bids us to "reckon yourselves to be dead indeed unto sin, but alive unto God through Jesus Christ," and to "yield yourselves unto God, as those that are alive from the dead, and your members as instruments of righteousness unto God."

Now, much of the teaching of the day would bid us yield ourselves unto God to be crucified and to die afresh, or more fully, but the Apostle says nothing of the kind here. On the contrary, we are to yield ourselves unto God as those who have already died and are alive from the dead, recognizing the cross as behind us; and for this very reason presenting ourselves to God, to be used for His service and glory. Have you never seen soaring in mid-heaven some glorious bird with its mighty pinions spread upon the bosom of the air and floating in the clear sky without a fluttering feather or apparently the movement of a muscle? It is poised in mid-air; floating yonder, far above the earth below; it does not need to rise, it has risen and is resting in its high and glorious altitude. Very different is the movement of the little lark that springs from the ground and, beating its wings in successive efforts, mounts up to the same aerial heights to sing its morning song, and then returning again to earth. One is the attitude of rising and the other is the attitude of risen.

Perhaps, you say, "How can I reckon myself dead when I find so many evidences that I am still alive, and how can I reckon myself risen when I find so many things that pull me back again to my lower plane? It is your failure to reckon and abide that drags you back. It is the recognizing of the old life as still alive that makes it real and keeps you from overcoming it. This is the principle which underlies the whole Gospel system, that we receive according to the reckoning of our faith. The magic wand of faith will lay all the ghosts that can rise in the cemetery of your soul; and the spirit of doubt will bring them up from the grave to haunt you as long as you continue to question. The only way you can ever die, is by surrendering yourself to Christ and then reckoning yourself dead with Him.

It is a portentous fact that spiritualism has power, apparently, to bring to life and to rehabilitate in the forms of flesh and blood the spirits of the dead. It is not an uncommon thing for a deceased father to appear to his child, and even speak to her in the old familiar tone, and tell of things that nobody could know but he, until the credulous mind is compelled to believe it is the same person, and that her buried father is truly alive. But it is not true. It is a lie. He is as dead as when you laid him in the tomb; his body is still there, corrupting in the ground, and his spirit is in the eternal world, although he seems to be alive. What does it mean? Why, it is one of the devil's lies. Satan has impersonated that father. He has supernatural power to paint upon the air the forms of those that have passed away, and to speak from those lips until they seem to be real. This is one of the mysteries and yet realities of the present day, and no wise or well informed man will attempt to dispute it. But the explanation is this: It is simply a creation of Satan before your senses to deceive you? What is the remedy? Refuse to recognize it. Reckon it dead. Tell it to its face, it is not your father, but one of the devil's brood, and it will immediately disappear. There is one thing Satan cannot stand and that is to be ignored and slighted. He lives on attention and dies of neglect. And so if you will refuse to recognize that manifestation of spiritualism, you will always find it disappears and has no power to continue its movements. It is wholly dependent on the consent of your will.

Now, here is a fine illustration of the principle of the Gospel. You surrender yourself unto Christ to be crucified with Him, and to have all your old life pass out, and henceforth to live as one born from heaven and animated by Him alone. Suddenly, some of your old traits of evil reappear, old thoughts, evil tendencies assert themselves and say loudly and clamorously, "We are not dead." Now if you recognize these things, fear them and obey them, you are sure to give them life and they will control you and drag you back into your former state. But if you refuse to recognize them, and say, "These are Satan's lies, I am dead indeed unto sin; these do not belong unto me, but are the children of the devil, I therefore repudiate them and rise above them," God will detach you from them and make them utterly dead. You will find they were no part of you, but simply temptations which Satan tried to throw over you, and to weave around you that which seemed part of yourself.

This is the true remedy for all the workings of temptation and sin. It is an awful fact that when one counts himself wicked he will become wicked. Let that pure girl be but made to believe that she is degraded and lost to virtue and she will have no heart to be pure, and she will recklessly sink to all the depths of sin! Let the child of God but begin to doubt his acceptance and expect to look upon his Father's face with a frown, and he will have no heart to be holy, he will sink into disobedience, discouragement and sin.

There is a strange story written by a gifted mind, describing a man who was two men alternately. When he believed himself to be a noble character, he was noble and true, and lived accordingly; but when the other ideal took possession of him and made him feel degraded, he went down accordingly. "As a man thinketh in his heart, so is he." Our reckonings reflect themselves in our realities; therefore, God has made this principle of faith to be the mainspring of personal righteousness and holiness, and the subtle, yet sublime, power that can lead men out of themselves into the very life of God.

Beloved, shall we let the Master teach us not so much to rise as to remember we are risen; that we have been raised with Christ from the dead, resurrected from the grave of our nothingness, and worse than nothingness, and that we are sitting with Him in heavenly places, recognized by the Father and permitted to reckon ourselves as being "even as he."

Our attitude will influence our aim. People live according to their standing. The high-born child of nobility carries in his bearing and his mien the consciousness of his noble descent, and so those who have their title to be on high, and are conscious of their high and heavenly rank, walk as children of the kingdom. The remainder of this chapter is devoted to working out this most practical idea, because we have risen with Christ, therefore let us live accordingly.

The argument against lying is: we have put off the old man and put on the new man. We have ceased to be paupers and become princes. Therefore, we are to put off the rags of the beggar and wear the epaulette of the prince. We have put on the new man, therefore, let us put on the kindness, humbleness of mind, meekness, long-suffering, and over all that charity, which is a perfect girdle that binds all the garments together. The best of all our robes is Christ Himself; and we are to put on Christ. This resurrection life is intensely practical. The Apostle brings it into touch with the nearest relationships of life, with the family circle, with the position of masters and servants, and with all the secular obligations of life. It is to affect our whole conduct and aims and lead us to walk wherever we are called.

This leads us to notice the practical power there is in this glorious fact, that we have been raised up together with Christ. It has power, in the first place, to confirm our hope and assurance of salvation because the resurrection of Jesus was the finishing work and a guarantee to men and angels that the ransom price was paid and the work of atonement complete. When Jesus came forth triumphant from the tomb, it was evident to the universe that the purpose for which He went there was fulfilled, the work He undertook satisfactorily done, and the Father satisfied with His finished atonement. Therefore, faith can rest upon His resurrection, as an everlasting foundation, and says: "Who is he that condemneth, It is Christ that died, yea rather, that is risen again."

Again, the resurrection of Christ is the power that sanctifies us. It enables us to count our old life, our former self, annihilated, so that we are no longer the same person in the eyes of God, or of ourselves; and we may with confidence repudiate ourselves and refuse either to obey or fear our former evil nature. Indeed, it is the risen Christ Himself who comes to dwell within us, and becomes in us the power of this new life and victorious obedience. It is not merely the fact of the resurrection, but the fellowship of the Risen One that brings us our victory and our power. We have learned the meaning of the sublime paradox, "I am crucified with Christ: nevertheless I live; yet not I, but Christ liveth in me." This is the only true and lasting sanctification, the indwelling life of Christ, the Risen One, in the believing and obedient soul.

Again, there is power in the resurrection to heal us. He that came forth from the tomb on that Easter morning was the physical Christ, and that body of His is the Head of our bodies, and the foundation of our physical strength, as well as our spiritual life. If we will receive and trust Him, He will do as much for our bodies as our spirits, and we shall find a new and supernatural strength in our mortal frame and the pulses of the future resurrection in our physical being.

Christ's resurrection has also a mighty power to energize our faith and encourage us to claim God's answers to our prayers, and ask difficult things from God. What can be too difficult or impossible after the open grave and the stone rolled away? God is trying to teach us the exceeding greatness of His power to us-ward "who believe, according to the working of his mighty power, Which he wrought in Christ when he raised him from the dead and set him at his own right hand." This is the measure of what God is able and willing to do in the name of Jesus under a Christian dispensation. Christ's resurrection is a pledge of all we can ask for, and if we fully believed in the power of that resurrection we would take much more than we have ever done.

The resurrection of the Lord Jesus Christ is the power for true service. The testimony of His resurrection is always peculiarly used by the Holy Spirit as the power of God unto the salvation of men. It was the chief theme of the ministry of the early apostles. They were always preaching of Jesus and the resurrection. It gives a peculiar brightness and attractiveness to Christian life and Christian work. Many Christians look as gloomy as if they were going to their own funeral. We heard not long ago of a little girl who met some sad looking people on the road and she said, "Mother, those are Christians, aren't they?" And when the mother asked her why she thought so, she said, "They look so unhappy."

This is the type of Christianity that comes from the cloister and the cross. This is not the Easter type, and certainly it is not the higher type. The religion of Jesus should be as bright as the blossoms of the spring, the songs of the warbling birds and the springing pulses of reviving nature. Our Lord met the women on that bright morning with the cheering message, "All hail," and so He would meet each one of us on the threshold of the year and the morning of a new Christian life and bid us go forth with the joy of our Lord as our strength.

This joy must spring from the resurrection and be maintained in a life beyond the grave, in the Heavenlies with its ascended Lord. This is the message that a sad and sinful world needs today. Its motto must not be the "Ecce homo" of the judgment hall, but the glad "All hail!" of the Easter dawn. The more of the indwelling Christ and the resurrection life in Christian work the more will be its living power to attract, sanctify and save the world.

Again, Christ's resurrection will enable us to meet the hardest places in life and endure its bitterest trials.

And so we read in Philippians that the power of His resurrection is to bring us into the fellowship of His sufferings, and make us conformable unto His death. We go into the resurrection life that we may be strong enough to suffer with Him and for Him.

Now, let there be no misunderstanding here. It does not mean that we are to suffer for ourselves through sickness or the struggles of our spiritual life. These sufferings ought to belong to the earlier period of our experiences. Our Lord had no conflicts about His sanctification and no physical disease to contend with during His life. So, in bearing these, we are not bearing the sufferings of Christ. Nay, His sufferings are for others and the power of His resurrection will bring us to share His high and holy sorrows for His suffering church and a dying world. It is a fact that the harder our place and the lower our sphere of toil and suffering the more do we need the elevation of His grace and glory to meet it. From the heights we must reach the depths. And, therefore, we find these epistles, which lift us into heavenly places, bring us back in every instance to the most commonplace duties, the most ordinary relationships and the most severe trials. These letters to the Ephesians and the Colossians which speak about the highest altitudes of faith and power, speak also more than any others of the temptations common to men, and the duties of husbands and wives, and the need of truthfulness, sobriety, honesty and righteousness, and all the most unromantic, practical experiences of human life.

There is a very remarkable passage in Isaiah which we have quoted above and which seems to be parallel with the thought in Philippians. It tells us of those that mount up with wings as eagles; but immediately afterward we find the same persons coming down to the ordinary walks of life, to run and not be weary, to walk and not faint. It would seem as if the mounting up was just intended to fit them for the running and walking, and that the higher experiences of grace and glory were just designed to enable them to tread the lower levels of toil and trial. It is in keeping with this that the apostle speaks of glorying in tribulation. "Glory" expresses the highest attitude of the soul, and "tribulation" the deepest degree of suffering. And so it would teach us that when we come to the deepest and lowest place we must meet it in the highest and most heavenly spirit. This is going down from the Mount of Transfiguration to meet the demoniac in the plain below, and cast out the power of Satan from a suffering world. Yes, these are the sufferings of Christ. The power of His resurrection is designed to prepare, enable us and help us to rise into all the heights of His glorious life, that like Him we may go forth to reflect it in blessing upon the lives of others, and find even sweeter joy in the ministrations of holy love than we have in the ecstasies of Divine communion.

Chapter 3

SAUL, OR SELF LIFE LEADING TO DESTRUCTION

The place of Saul in Old Testament history is significant and, we believe, typical of great spiritual truths. It is conceded that Israel's redemption from Egypt foreshadowed human redemption through the cross of Calvary and the finished work of Christ. It is also beyond question that the triumph of Joshua and the conquest of Canaan pointed forward to the Pentecostal baptism and blessing of the Apostolic church and the deeper rest into which the Holy Ghost brings the individual Christian.

The dark period of declension recorded in the book of Judges and the earlier chapters of Samuel were typical of the dark ages of Christianity, and the Reformation under Samuel was strongly parallel to our Protestant Reformation and the revival of the church of Christ from the bondage of mediaeval darkness and superstition. A little farther on we shall find that the kingdom of David and Solomon was the type of Christ's Millennial throne.

But what was the meaning of the strange parenthesis of Saul's life that came before the kingdom of David and Samuel? Alas! it is the counterfeit kingdom which Satan is seeking to set up on the throne of human selfishness and worldly pride, instead of the true kingdom of the Lord Jesus Christ, and of which, alas! we have too many evidences in the compromising and worldly ecclesiasticism of our day, and in the Laodicean picture which the Apocalypse has given of the church that is to be rejected at the coming of the Lord.

But while this is the dispensational meaning of Saul's life, it has a still more solemn personal application for every individual Christian. It is God's fearful object lesson of the power and peril of the self life and the need of its utter crucifixion before we can enter into the true kingdom of spiritual victory and power.

1. We see the spirit of self in the very motive that prompted the kingdom of Saul. Samuel perfectly understood it as a virtual rejection of God as the supreme King of Israel and a real vain-glorious desire to be independent of Divine control and to be like the surrounding nations of the world. "Make us a king," they said, "to judge us like all the nations." No wonder that Samuel was deeply displeased and prayed unto

the Lord, but God answered him: "Hearken unto the voice of the people in all that they say unto thee: for they have not rejected thee, but they have rejected me, that I should not reign over them."

Nevertheless, Samuel still protested and solemnly warned them of the burdens and the exactions which their king would claim from them and the trouble they were bringing upon themselves, adding: "Ye shall cry out in that day because of your king which ye shall have chosen you; and the Lord will not hear you in that day." But it was no use. They had set their heart upon their king and they answered: "We will have a king over us; That we also may be like all the nations; and that our king may judge us, and go out before us, and fight our battles." This is the spirit of the prodigal, saying, "Father, give me the portion of goods that falleth to me." It is the desire of independence which is the very root of human sin, and it is the spirit of conformity to the world into which self life always develops. We see it in the spirit of worldly conformity in the church today, and we are conscious of it in our own natural hearts as that broad, self-asserting and dominant 'I' which makes man a God unto himself and refuses to surrender his will to Christ, or yield the direction of his life to the will of God and the government of the Holy Ghost.

Therefore, the very first step in the new life must ever be surrender; and the essential condition of the baptism of the Holy Ghost is to yield the very last point to God, and even the things which may in themselves be harmless must be first surrendered if for no other reason than to prove our will is wholly laid down, and that God is all in all.

2. We see the spirit of self in the character of Saul, and the qualifications which made him the choice and the idol of the people. Saul was the very embodiment of the human. He represented all that was most strong, chivalrous, attractive and promising in human nature. He was of splendid physique, a head taller than all the people, a magnificent specimen of physical manhood, and "every inch a king."

He possessed the intellectual, moral and social qualities that constitute a great public leader. He was brave, heroic, enthusiastic and generous, and the early years of his reign are adorned with some stirring examples of heroic deeds. He was all that the human heart would choose. He represented the best possibilities of human nature, and as the people looked at his splendid figure they shouted again and again that patriotic cry which has so often reechoed since, and which has so seldom been fulfilled as a prayer to heaven, "God save the king."

God had to let this man stand before the ages to show that man at his best is only man and that human self-sufficiency must end in failure and desperate sorrow. This is the lesson that God is trying to teach His children still. How few of them have found it out so fully that they can say, "I know that in me, that is, in my flesh, dwelleth no good thing." The sentence of death has passed upon the flesh, and there is but one thing that we can do with it – to nail it to the cross of Jesus Christ, to reckon it dead, and to keep it forever in His bottomless grave.

3. The spirit of self in Saul was combined with much that was good and attractive, both naturally and spiritually. Naturally, we have seen that he was not only a man of princely bearing, but of many noble and heroic qualities. He had also a most beautiful family, and Jonathan, his son, is the most attractive figure in the long gallery of Bible characters.

When Saul came to Samuel and was first called to the kingdom he seemed to have many elements of sterling virtue and genuine humility. Like a dutiful son, he went to search for his father's asses, and then he went to the prophet Samuel to ask counsel about finding them. When he came to Samuel and was told his extraordinary message and anointed to be king there was no unbecoming self-consciousness about him. He kept his secret with discretion and modesty, and even in telling his uncle about the words of Samuel, he said nothing to him about the greater message concerning the kingdom. When he left the presence of Samuel he did just what he was told, and when he met the company of prophets he joined them and received a real baptism of the Spirit like them, and prophesied among them with genuine religious enthusiasm. And even when they sought for him to bring him out before the people and announce to him their choice as the national ruler, they could not find him, for he was hiding among the stuff and he seemed a very paragon of modesty and unobtrusiveness. And yet this was the very man who let the dark and dreadful shadow of himself blight his own life and ruin his kingdom and his family. Oh, how self-deceptive is the human spirit. Oh, how pride itself will hide away in the very guise of deepest humility! In speaking of his earlier life the prophet Samuel pays a tribute to his earlier humility. "When thou wast little in thine own sight," he says, "wast thou not made the head of the tribes of Israel, and the Lord anointed thee king over Israel?" We cannot doubt that Samuel's language is perfectly sincere, and that he is giving Saul credit for at least a measure of genuine humility. What then was the defect? May it have been this? It is one thing to be little in our own eyes, it is another thing to be out of our own sight altogether. True humility is not thinking meanly of ourselves, it is not thinking of ourselves at all. What we need is not so much self-denial as self-crucifixion and utter self-forgetfulness. The perfect child is just as unconscious in the highest place as in the lowest, and the true spirit of Christ in us recognizes ourselves as no longer ourselves, but so one with the Lord Jesus that we may truly say: "Not I, but Christ liveth in me." "By the grace of God I am what I am."

But what are we to learn from this combination of so many excellencies in one life and its ultimate failure and ruin? Alas, we are to learn that Satan's choicest wile is to mingle the good with the evil and to cover his poison as a sugar-coated pill, because he knows we would never take it in its unmixed and undiluted evil. Satan's choicest agents are those that are attractive and naturally lovely. Esau was a more winning man naturally than Jacob; but Esau was lost and Jacob was chosen. You may be beautiful, you may be wise, you may be cultured, you may be moral, you may be useful, you may be noble and generous, and yet, withal, you may be living for yourself and, at last, like Saul, be self-destroyed. Satan doesn't want your property outright now; he only wants a mortgage on it, and he is content to take a mortgage for a thousand dollars if he cannot get one for a hundred thousand. He can wait for the day of foreclosure. All he wants is to have his hand in it. It is the mixed lives that are doing the mischief.

"Wherefore come ye out from among them, and be ye separate, saith the Lord, and touch not the unclean thing; and I will receive you, And will be a Father unto you, and ye shall be my sons and daughters, saith the Lord Almighty."

4. The first test came to Saul in an hour of severe trial when, beleaguered by his enemies and deserted by almost all his soldiers, he seemed to be facing destruction. Waiting seven days for Samuel to come and begin the battle by the usual sacrificial offering, Saul at last grew discouraged and impatient, and then he presumed to take upon himself the priestly functions which belonged only to Samuel, and to offer up the sacrifice without waiting for the prophet. As he was offering it, Samuel came and instantly pronounced upon Saul the terrible sentence: "Thou hast done foolishly: thou hast not kept the commandment of the LORD thy God, which He commanded thee: for now would the LORD thy God have established thy kingdom upon Israel forever. But now thy kingdom shall not continue: the LORD hath sought him a man after his own heart, and the LORD hath commanded

him to be captain over his people, because thou hast not kept that which the Lord commanded thee."

Many a life succeeds while all is successful, but in the hour of trial self always shows itself. Saul was a splendid king until the first great trial met him, and then he became discouraged, distrustful, self-asserting and presumptuous, and dared to take in his own hands the things that belonged only to God. He usurped the throne of God Himself and showed his true nature. He was a man of his own heart and not of God's heart, and henceforth God sought Him a man after God's heart who should do God's will and not his own, and thus be a true representative of Israel's true King.

As soon as Saul had shown himself in his real character, God immediately delivered the people out of their peril by two feeble men – Jonathan and his armorbearer – that He might show to Saul how little he needed his strength or any human strength or wisdom, and how all-sufficient God was to those who truly trusted Him. Even this victory Saul almost wrecked by his interference and wilfulness, and it became apparent by his own folly that he could not be trusted with God's work, and that his persistent self-will would always hinder the will and the work of God.

Not instantly did the crisis come. God let this spirit of self work out to its full development slowly; but it was evident from this hour that Saul's life must fail, and that Samuel's prophecy was, alas, true.

5. God gave another opportunity and second test. He sent Saul on an important expedition to destroy Amalek, the race of Esau that had tried to hinder Israel in their passage through the wilderness. There is a deep spiritual meaning back of this story; for Amalek was a type of the flesh; and the destruction of Amalek was just an illustration of the very principle which Saul's life so strongly emphasizes, and Saul's failure to destroy Amalek is, therefore, the more significant because it shows how deeply rooted the self-principle was in his own soul. The man who spared Agag was the man who spared the principle of self in his own heart; and the two pictures blend with an awful significance for everyone of us.

Saul successfully accomplished the invasion and returned victorious. He even seems to have been so possessed with the spirit of self-complacency that he failed to realize his own true character until Samuel uttered his fearful words of doom. "Yea, I have obeyed the voice of the Lord," he cried with perfect assurance, and when the awful words of the prophet answered back: "To obey is better than sacrifice, and to hearken than the fat of rams. . . . Because thou hast rejected the word of the Lord, he hath also rejected thee from being king"; it is doubtful if even then Saul fully realized the nature of his sin. So subtle and self-deceiving is the spirit of self that even then all he seemed to feel was the fear of being humiliated before the people, and he begged the petty bauble of Samuel's public recognition and honor, and this little bit of vainglory was the solace and the comfort of his wretched soul in the hour when the sentence of death and ruin was thundering in his ears.

What a spectacle of complacent self-deception; the snare of a religious motive, keeping the spoil to sacrifice to the Lord! We see the fear of man, the unwillingness of this weak man to displease the people when they begged him to save the precious booty of Amalek.

But one word above all others seems to crystallize the very element of this stupendous folly. It is the word "compromise." Saul obeyed, but with a compromise. Saul did much good, but he compromised with evil. God's commandments are uncompromising, inexorable, unqualified, and our obedience must be inflexible, absolute and complete. The faintest reservation is really the very soul of disobedience. The failure even to hearken to the full meaning of God indicates a spirit of unwilling obedience.

Saul stands before us in this picture the incarnation

of self-will and, therefore, the enemy of God, nay, the rival of God upon His very throne. Could there be any other issue? "Thou hast rejected the word of the Lord, and the Lord hath rejected thee from being king."

6. Not immediately did the judgment culminate. Slowly still, the coil of self unwinds until all its hidden sinuosities have been revealed. Saul did much work after this, much good work, fought many battles, fought them well, reigned over Israel, and established a powerful kingdom, but it was Saul's kingdom and not God's. All the remaining years were years of self-activity and self-vindication. For nine years he pursued David, his rival, with ferocious hate. The Spirit of God left him, and an evil spirit, by God's permission, possessed him; and as the years went on, the beginning and the end of his existence was Saul and not Jehovah. It was self-incarnate with all its miserable works and fruits.

7. At last the culmination came. Eaten out by the canker of self, his heart became the dwelling place of Satan. The devil took entire possession of him, and in one dreadful hour he gave himself up to spiritualism, and, rejected of the Lord, sought the counsel of necromancers, whom he had formerly persecuted and banished from his kingdom. It was the last fatal step. Self had driven God from his throne, and now it gave it

41

to Satan and the next chapter of self life was self-destruction.

Trembling and prostrated by the fearful vision which his own presumption had brought up from the depths of Hades, Saul dashed with reckless despair into the last battle of his life, and the next day the tragedy was complete – the flower of Israel's youth was lying on the slopes of Gilboa – the army of Saul was annihilated – the Philistines were victorious on every side – the kingdom which Saul had built up for a quarter of a century for himself was broken to pieces and scattered to the winds – Saul's sons were lying dead on the mountain sides, and Saul himself, a wretched suicide, had gone to his own place. The scorpion, self, had stung others, and now, at last, it stung itself to death. The revelation of human selfishness was complete, and before the sad and fearful spectacle we may well stand in awe and humbly, earnestly and fervently pray:

> Oh, to be saved from myself, dear Lord,
> Oh, to be lost in Thee!
> Oh, that it might be no more I,
> But Christ that lives in me.

Chapter 4

AGAG, OR THE SUBTLETIES OF THE SELF LIFE

"Then said Samuel, Bring ye hither to me Agag, the king of the Amalekites. And Agag came unto him delicately. And Agag said, Surely the bitterness of death is past. And Samuel said, As thy sword hath made women childless, so shall thy mother be childless among women. And Samuel hewed Agag in pieces before the Lord at Gilgal." (1 Sam. 15: 32, 33).

WE HAVE already referred to this passage as an illustration of the character of Saul. There is still a deeper type of the subtleties of the self life in the picture of Agag which the Holy Ghost has framed into the narrative of this solemn history. Saul and Agag both teach the same great lesson and warning, namely, the peril of a self-centered life, but they teach it in somewhat different ways, and the story of Agag is worthy of our prayerful and heart-searching consideration.

1. His Race. He belonged to the race of Amalek and the family of Esau, who represent through their entire

genealogy the life of the flesh. From the very beginning of the human race God has drawn the line of demarcation between two races – the fleshly and the spiritual man. Just outside the gate of Eden the division began. The family of Seth called themselves by the name of the Lord, and the race of Cain went off and built their city of culture and pride and became the pioneers of the worldliness and wickedness adorned and ameliorated by all the grace of human culture and all the attractions of earthly delight. The separation, alas, soon began to disappear and in the days of Noah the two races had mingled and intermarried, and the progeny was a generation of monsters of iniquity so degenerate and depraved that God turned with loathing from the whole race and pronounced the awful sentence, "The end of all flesh is come before me; I will destroy them with the earth."

After the flood God chose a separate family, the line of Abraham, and again endeavored to keep the chosen people separate. All along that line we see the earthly off-shoots of the family-tree separating from the central trunk and going out into the world. The first of these was Ishmael, the type of the spirit of bondage and sin. The next of these was Esau, the progenitor of a whole race who inherited the earthly spirit of their father, who, for a morsel of meat, sold his birthright and afterwards married with the daughters of Canaan and became as corrupt and polluted as they. In the same line were the descendants of Lot's unnatural daughters, the Moabites and the Ammonites.

Above all these, the race of Esau and Amalek were the representatives of the spirit of the flesh and the world. This was the reason that God pronounced the decree of their extermination. We find that when Israel went out of Egypt and started on their journey through the wilderness on their way to the Land of Promise, Amalek was the first to attack them. It is not difficult to see in this the foreshadowing of the fact that the first adversary that we have to contend with when we leave our sinful past of bondage and iniquity is the carnal nature in our own hearts, which soon asserts itself and tries to force us back to "the gall of bitterness, and in the bond of iniquity." This is what Agag represents and this is what each of us has found to our cost to be a very real element in the experience of a Christian life.

2. The name of Agag is next significant. It is from the root "Hak," which is a generic form denoting, like Pharaoh, a ruler. It literally means ruler, and represents the spirit of self-will, self-assertion and independence in the human heart. Its prototype is Lucifer, the prince of light and glory, who, being lifted up with pride and refusing to be controlled, turned from an angel to a

fiend, and has become the desperate leader of the rebellious hosts of hell. We see it next in the supreme temptation of the Fall – "Ye shall be as gods" – the desire for supremacy. We see it in the spirit of human ambition, in the Oriental despot, in the world conqueror, in the society belle and the political "boss." All belong to the same family. They are of the race of Amalek and the house of Agag. Their cry is like the prodigal, "Give me the portion of goods that falleth to me" and let me go away from parental control and do as I please.

There is no country where it is so rampant as our own. It appears to us as young mannishness and calls itself liberty, but its end is license, lawlessness and Anti-Christ, that Lawless one who is yet to embody the elements of human wickedness and pride, and end the present dispensation by defying God and man and perishing, like his father, the devil, in his presumptuous pride. This spirit is found in every human heart. It may be disguised in many insidious forms. It may call itself by illustrious names and ape the highest ambitions and the noblest pretensions, but it is Agag and Satan every time. The thing in you that wants to rule, wants to have its own way, to be independent, refuse control, to despise reproof, is wrong in its very nature. The very first thing you need in order to be of any use anywhere is to be thoroughly broken, completely subjected and utterly crucified in the very core and center of your will. Then you will accept discipline and learn to yield and obey in matters in themselves indifferent and your will, will be so merged in His that He can use you as a flexible and perfectly adjusted instrument, and henceforth you shall will only what God wills and choose only what God chooses for you.

This is the real battleground of human salvation; this is the Waterloo of every soul; this is the test question of every redeemed life. This was the point where Saul lost his kingdom and Agag lost his life, and where still the eternal destinies are lost or won as we learn the lesson or refuse to be led in triumph by our conquering Lord.

Beloved, let us mark it well. Let us not miss the warning. Let us remember forever that no man can rule others until he himself is absolutely led of God, that no man can conquer foes till he first is conquered, that no man can lead in triumph the hosts of evil or the hearts of men until he himself is led in triumph the willing captive of the Savior's love and the Master's will.

3. The Decree of Extermination. God has determined that the race of Amalek and the house of Agag should be utterly exterminated. They were not to be spared, but to be destroyed. It was a case of no compromise.

There was nothing good in them. The least element of Agagism was destructive and the whole community, with all their goods and belongings, must be put out of existence. Now, this is God's decree against the flesh in us. It cannot be cleansed. It cannot be improved. It cannot be cultivated. It cannot be educated into ideas and principles. It must be exterminated. Now, what is the flesh? Is it the bad principle in man? Is it some outward or inward evil which can be cut away like a tumor by a surgical operation? Listen, "The carnal mind is enmity against God: for it is not subject to the law of God, neither indeed can be. So then they that are in the flesh cannot please God." There is the uncompromising decree of the total depravity and the hopeless condition of the flesh. But now what is the flesh? Listen again: "But ye are not in the flesh, but in the Spirit, if so be that the Spirit of God dwell in you." There is the distinction clear as a ray of celestial light. Every man who has not the spirit of God is in the flesh, therefore, everything outside the spirit of God is flesh. Therefore, the flesh is not simply the sinful part of human nature, but the whole of human nature. It is the Adamic race. It is the natural man. It is the whole creature, and the whole thing is corrupt and polluted. The tree is so crooked you cannot straighten it without cutting it in two. The tumor is so interwoven with the

48

flesh that you cannot cut it without killing the man. There is no remedy. There is no hope. The old life must be laid down and the new creation, wholly born out of heaven and baptized with the Spirit of God, must take its place as a resurrected life, as a new creation, as an experience so supernatural and Divine that its possessor can truly say, "I am no longer the former man, I have died and Christ has taken my place. It is no longer I, but Christ that liveth in me."

Don't try to sanctify the flesh. Don't attempt to evolve the kingdom of heaven out of the kingdom of hell. It is not evolution, it is creation. It is not morals or manners, it is a miracle of grace and power. Take no risks upon the old man. He will fail you every time. You may think your trained hawk is a dove, but in an unsuspecting moment its beak will be buried in your flesh. Your little wolf may have all the manners of the lamb, but in an evil hour it will destroy all your lambs and perhaps rend you limb from limb. It is hopelessly, eternally corrupt. It cannot please God. It must be utterly dethroned, renounced and crucified with Christ.

4. We see next the attempt of man to compromise with the flesh and to disregard this Divine decree of its extermination. Saul spared Agag that he might grace his triumph, and he kept the best of the spoil that he

might sacrifice unto the Lord his God. He obeyed the commandment of the Lord to a certain extent. He defeated Amalek and destroyed the nation in a sense. He did all God told him as far as it was agreeable, and he took his own way just where it was pleasant. His obedience, therefore, was not really obedience to God, but truly self-will. He retained just enough of the flesh to destroy the whole service. The very essence of the disobedience was compromise. The very worst thing about it was that he tried to put the evil to a good use. It was a very insult in the face of heaven to bring the forbidden thing and offer it to the God he had defied. Now this is just the spirit of modern religious culture. Don't go too far. Don't be extreme. Don't be puritanical. Go easy. Be liberal. Meet the world half way. Marry that scoundrel to save him. Take that saloon keeper into the church because you can make good use of his money. Put that brazen-faced woman up in the choir because she will draw her theatrical set to hear her sing. Go to the theater and the play with your husband to get him to go to church with you on Sunday.

Nonsense. In the first place, in such an unequal contest on the enemy's ground the devil will always get the best of you, and instead of being saved the husband will drag to his level the woman that ventured on forbidden ground. The operatic singer, instead of

50

bringing her set under the influence of religion, will bring the church to the level of her set and turn it into a clubhouse and a concert-room. The saloon keeper's money will moderate the tone of the preaching so that it will be a comfort unto Sodom, and vice and sin can sit unchecked, and even count itself the very buttress and pillar of the cause of the holy Christ.

Think you that God will accept such service? Will He who owns the treasures of the universe and could create a mountain or a mine of gold in a moment, and send a thousand angels to sing in His sanctuaries, will He accept the money that is stained with the blood of souls and polluted with the filth of dethroned purity and honor? Will He accept the meretricious service that is sold for sordid gain? Will He go begging to the devil's shrine, and asking his permission to let go his captives that they may be saved? Shame upon our unfaithfulness and our compromise! Oh, for the sword of a Samuel to hew in pieces the compromises that are an offence to heaven and a disgrace to the Bride of the Lamb.

5. We see the fawning pleading of the flesh for indulgence. Agag came forth, walking delicately, mincing like a silly, coquettish girl, smiling, seeking by his blandishments to disarm opposition, to win favor, looking like an incarnation of gentleness and

innocence. A perfect gentleman! Surely, he could not harm a child! Surely, no one could dream of doing him harm! Ah, that is the old flesh pleading for his life, pointing out its refinement, its culture, its graces, the good that it is doing and wants to do, its claim upon your consideration and regard. It will decorate your church with the finest taste; it will sing in your choirs with all the harmonies of classical music and attract crowds; it will bring society to your church; it will give you a bright and liberal theology. It is full of humanitarian plans for the relief of the suffering and the uplifting of degradation, and it offers you a Pullman palace car prepaid to the gates of heaven.

Surely, such a beautiful gentle creature should not be rudely slain. But back of all its disguises and fawning, the Holy Ghost will show you, if you will let Him, the serpent's coil, the dragon's voice and the festering corpse of the charnel house.

Death is not always repulsive at the first sight. The daughter of Jairus was beautiful in her shroud, and a flush of life still lingered on her cheek, but she was as dead as Lazarus festering in his tomb. And so that sweet-faced girl, with her fawning charms, that brilliant minister with his intellectual sophistries, that voice that sings like an angel in the choir, are as corrupt and polluted as that poor creature that lies in yonder hospital dropping to pieces in the last stages of corruption, or that red-handed assassin reeking with the blood of his victim. They are both flesh, only at different stages of their moral putrefaction.

6. We see in Agag the flesh feigning death. "Surely," said Agag, "the bitterness of death is past." And so you will find plenty of people in pulpits and pews, on platforms and in obscure corners, who would make you believe that they are utterly dead, and yet who remind you when you get a good look at them of corpses walking around in their grave clothes. They are so conscious of their deadness that you know they are alive. They are so proud of their humility that you would rather they were proud than humble. They are so constantly in their own shadow that they try you by their religious egotism. Surely, dead people don't know it, don't think about it, are unostentatious, unobtrusive, modest, simple, natural, free, and, like good water, without taste, color or consciousness. Oh, for this blessed simplicity and this place of self-forgetting rest! Oh, for this fulfillment of the prayer, "Lord, let me die so dead that I won't know it."

Beloved, there is no danger so great, especially among Christians somewhat advanced, as that of counting ourselves in a place where we really do not live. There is nothing so hardening to the heart as to take the place of self-surrender and then live a life of self-indulgence, self-will and adding to it the greater fault of self-complacency; calling things holy which are not, bringing the standard down to our own experience and filling ourselves with a self-complacent dream. Truly, we are to reckon that we are dead indeed. We are not to reckon that we are reckoned dead, but we are to reckon on a reality, and we are to insist upon it and take nothing less from God or from ourselves. Oh, that we would dare to call things by their right names and have no counterfeit, even from ourselves.

7. We see self exposed and slain. Agag could not deceive Samuel. The old man pierces him through with one glance of the Holy Ghost, and looking at his mincing, fawning figure, we can imagine him saying, "I know you with all your fawning. You are an old murderer. You are a selfish, cruel tyrant. Your sword has made many a mother childless, many an innocent victim has been crushed beneath your lust or hate, and back of all your smiles there is a skeleton and a serpent's sting." And then with that sharp sword he cut through his blandishments and hewed him to pieces before the Lord.

Sin never stops till it reaches its worst, and God shows us in a single sample the possibilities of the evil to which the tiniest seed and fairest bud of selfishness may yet ripen.

Beloved, let us ask God to expose it in our hearts. Let us open our being to the sword of Samuel, which is just the sword of the Holy Ghost. It is described in the Epistle to the Hebrews in these solemn, searching, but blessed words: "The Word of God is quick, and powerful, and sharper than any two-edged sword, piercing even to the dividing asunder of soul and spirit, and of the joints and marrow, and is a discerner of the thoughts and intents of the heart."

All that we need to be delivered from any form of self and sin is to really be willing to see it, to recognize it, to call it by its right name, to throw off its disguise, to brand it with its true character, to pass sentence of death upon it, to stand to the sentence without cornpromise, to consent to no reprieve, to give God the right to slay it, and then there is power enough in the sword of the Spirit, in the fire of the Holy Ghost, in the blood of Calvary, in the faithfulness and love and grace of God to make us dead indeed unto sin, but alive unto God through Jesus Christ our Lord.

Chapter 5

JONAH, OR THE SHADOW OF SELF

"Therefore now, O Lord, take, I beseech thee, my life from me; it is better for me to die than to live." (Jonah 4: 3).

This was the best prayer that Jonah ever uttered, if he had only really meant it in the right sense. The greatest need of Jonah's life was to die to Jonah, and his life is just a great object lesson of the odiousness and the foolishness of the spirit of selfishness in any mortal, especially in anyone who professes, or pretends, to work for God and the souls of men. Selfishness is always odious and out of place; but it is never so much so as it is in the man who professes to represent a crucified Redeemer and a loving God.

The story of Jonah is soon told. He was the first of the prophets whose writings have come down to us in the sacred canon. He lived in the reign of Jeroboam II, and it was through his instrumentality that that powerful monarch was enabled to raise Israel from the deep depression into which the nation had fallen, and restore her to the highest point of power and greatness in all the history of the nation.

56

Sent as the prophet of good tidings to his own people, he gladly went and by his inspired messages cheered on his countrymen, until they had subdued their enemies on every side, and won back their long lost territory from all their foes.

Had Jonah's career terminated at this point he would have gone into history as one of the most successful and brilliant of Israel's long line of splendid prophets. But God gave him a new commission, and sent him unexpectedly with a message of warning to the city of Nineveh, the mighty capital of the Assyrian Empire. This was to Jonah most unexpected and unwelcome. An enthusiastic patriot, he did not want to do anything that could bring the favor of God to the hated enemies of his country. And so the whole self-will of the man rose up in rebellion, and he determined not to go. Disobedience always brings separation from God, and so Jonah was inevitably driven from the presence of God, and looked about for some place where he might escape from the All-Seeing Eye whose glance he could not bear.

It was not difficult to find a chain of providences all working in the direction he wanted to go. And finding a ship at Joppa bound for the coast of distant Tarshish, he secured a passage at once and started for the chosen hiding-place. He was soon overtaken by the

57

messengers of God's mercy and judgment, and, thrown into the sea as a sacrifice to appease the storm, he was swallowed by the great fish which God had prepared, and then thrown out from his living tomb, a resurrected man, where God's message met him again – his commission was renewed to go to Nineveh, and preach the preaching that God commanded.

This time he went without any evasions or questionings, and for a time it really seemed that he was indeed a crucified man. But alas for human self-assertion! It was not long before Jonah came to the surface again. As long as his work succeeded and the people listened and repented, he was satisfied; but when God, in His mercy, met the penitence of the Ninevites with His mercy, and cancelled His judgment upon them, Jonah was bitterly disappointed and fiercely angry because his reputation as a prophet had been ruined by the failure of his threatenings; and sitting down under the shade of a gourd outside the city gates he fretted and scolded like a petulant and angry child, and finally he passes out of sight altogether, under his withered gourd, as a spectacle of humiliation and contempt, all the glory of his really wonderful work blighted by the dark shadow of himself which he threw over it in his egregious folly and unspeakable selfishness.

There are many lessons taught us by this extraordinary life.

1. We see a man who succeeds most wonderfully in religious work, so long as his work is congenial, but fails completely and utterly breaks down under the first severe test of real character. Jonah did splendid work so long as everything went all right; but the moment things went against him, he went to pieces. How many of us there are who in the sunshine of religious prosperity seem to be extraordinary workers and even ideal saints. It is the test that tells. Character is more than work, and God is leading us, if we will only let Him, through the tests which will bring us to the death of self, and to the place where He can use us as

> Only His messengers ready,
> His praises to sound at His will,
> Or willing should He not require us
> In silence to wait on Him still.

2. We see in him a man who obeys and serves God as long as it suits him, but is a stranger to that obedience which knows no choice except the Master's will. "Ye are my friends," the Master says, "if ye do whatsoever I command you." It is no evidence of friendship to Christ to do some things to please Him, to

59

do much that is good and right; the true friend does whatsoever He commands.

3. We see in Jonah a man destitute of the true missionary spirit, a man who thought he was full of zeal, yet had no real love for God or the souls of men. Jehu had zeal enough, but it was zeal for his own cause. Jonah represents those people who will work as hard as you please for their own cause, even for the church, and the work which centers in their own sect, or family or country, but they know nothing of the real missionary spirit. They care not for the Ninevites, the Chinese, or the Africans, and they think it unreasonable waste to pour out our hundreds of thousands of dollars for the evangelization of the world, instead of spending it at home, and using it to promote the welfare of our own people.

4. A man running away from God. When we disobey God, we shall soon want to leave His presence altogether. Adam's single sin soon led to Adam's separation from his Creator, and we find him hiding from the presence of God. It is idle to think that you can indulge in any act of disobedience, and still look up in your Father's face and call yourself His child.

Jonah had no difficulty in finding means to carry on his purpose. The devil has his providences as well as the Lord. The ship was all ready, and it was going to the right place, and Jonah was soon on board, and comfortably asleep in his berth. Alas, the saddest thing about backsliding is, that it brings with it the devil's sedatives, and the soul can calmly sleep amid the fiercest storm, and complacently dream that all is well. There is nothing in all the judgments of God so terrible as a reprobate mind and a soul past feeling.

5. A man pursued by God's police, and brought to his senses by the trials and troubles which he brings upon himself and others. Thank God for the mercy that will not let us rest in our self-complacency and sin. Happy for us that we have a Father who loves us well enough to hurt us and drive us home to His loving breast. The saddest part of the trouble of the back-slider is, that he brings it upon others, and that he has to suffer because of the backslider's sin and folly.

Jonah's shipmates were the first to feel the effects of his disobedience, and to wake him up from his fool-hardy insensibility. Many a time it is not until our fortunes have been wrecked, and our families brokenhearted, that we find out the secret of all our troubles, and come back to Him who has smitten only that He might heal us, and broken only that He might bind us up.

What a pity that we should compel God to bring us back to Himself by the officers of judgment, instead of flying to the arms of His love, and choosing the blessing which He is determined we shall not lose.

6. We see in Jonah a man who had to die to himself before he could do any real good.

The great lesson of Jonah's life is the need of crucifixion to the life of self. Our Savior has used the story of Jonah as the special type of His own death and resurrection, and we know that our Savior's cross is the pattern of ours, and that as He died, so we should die to the life of self and sin.

In the story of Jonah we see God lovingly slaying the selfish prophet, and trying to put Jonah out of his own way, so that God could bless him as He really wanted to. Surely, if ever a man had a good chance to die, it was Jonah, and if he didn't, it was his own fault. He speaks of that living tomb himself as the belly of Hades – the very bosom of death, and the prayer that he uttered, when in those awful depths, certainly sounded like the voice of a man who meant what he said; and when he came forth, it really did seem as if the old Jonah was going to be out of the picture henceforth. But alas! As we shall see later, he was only half dead yet. God cannot use any but a crucified man to preach about the crucified Savior.

When Jonah came forth from the depths of death he was ready to go anywhere that God wanted him, and when we are dead to self and sin we will not have any question to ask except this one: "Lord, what wilt thou have me to do?" Then we will go to Nineveh, or China, or any place the Master sends us, with glad and willing hearts.

7. But we see in Jonah a man who, after all, was only half dead, notwithstanding all his suffering and humiliation.

For a time he goes right on faithful and obedient. He preaches to the Ninevites the preaching that God bids him, and the most wonderful revival that ever attended any ministry follows his words, until from the king on the throne to the meanest of his subjects, the people of Nineveh are prostrate at the feet of Jehovah, and pleading for mercy.

But the moment that God hears their cry and disappoints Jonah's predictions of their destruction, the prophet breaks completely down and falls into a fit of petulance and anger, because God had failed to do what he had threatened and destroyed his reputation as a prophet.

It was but another form of the same old self life. A man may give up the selfishness that its gratification in the pleasures of the world, and yet may seek the gratification of the same self life in some religious form. A woman may cease to be the queen of

63

society and the idol of her hero worshipers, yet she may drink in the sweet delight of her influence and sway over the minds and hearts of men, in her very work for Christ, and the influence that she wields over the hearts that she brings under her religious sway.

The orator, as he holds spellbound the hearts of thousands, even when he tells them of Jesus and salvation, may be just as selfish and self-conscious as the actor on the stage, or the politician on the rostrum who speaks only for his personal triumph and ambition. Jonah's very success was his snare, and led him to forget his Master's glory and the real good of the people that he was sent to save, in thinking of his own success and his own glory.

God never can use any man very much till he has grace enough to forget himself entirely while doing God's work; for He will not give His glory to another nor share with the most valued instrument the praise that belongs to Jesus Christ alone.

We can never succeed in our service for God till we learn to cast our own shadow behind us and lose ourselves in the honor and glory of our Master. It is said that Alexander the Great had a famous horse that nobody could ride. Alexander at length attempted to tame him. He saw at a glance that the horse was afraid of his own shadow, and so, leaping into the saddle one day and turning the horse's head to the sun, he struck his spurs into the flanks of the noble steed, and dashed off like the lightning. From that hour the fiery charger was thoroughly subdued, and he never gave his master any trouble again. He could no longer see his own shadow.

Oh, that we could look into the face of our Lord, and then forever forget ourselves! Then He could use us for His own glory and afford to share with us the glory and gladness of our work.

8. We see in Jonah a man whom God had to humble in the dust to save him from destroying his own work.

God loves to make us partakers with Him in the fruits of our work. So He honored Moses and Samuel and Paul, and their names have come down to us associated with their blessed service for the Master; but this was because they loved to forget themselves, and seek only their Master's glory. How different it was with poor Jonah! He was seeking his own glory, and God had to humiliate him, and let him fail altogether in the very thing he wanted. Surely, "God resisteth the proud, but giveth grace unto the humble." Surely, he that would be chiefest may well become the servant of all; for the Master has said, "If any man will come after me, let him deny himself, and take up his cross, and follow me. For whosoever will save his life shall lose it:

and whosoever will lose his life for my sake shall find it." "If any man serve me, let him follow me; ... if any man serve me, him will my Father honor."

Poor Jonah lost this honor, because he sought it, and Paul found it, because he renounced it, and sought only to live that Jesus might be satisfied, even if Paul should be forever forgotten. This is the spirit of true service, and surely this is the solemn lesson that comes down to us through that humiliating spectacle, sitting, disappointed and rejected under his withered gourd, after the most successful ministry ever given to a human life, but one which brought no recompense to him, because he did it for himself.

9. We see in Jonah the picture of a man who wants to die when he is least prepared to die.

It was a very great mercy that God refused to take him at his word, when he cried with childish petulance, "Lord, I beseech thee, take away my life from me; for it is better for me to die than to live." Let us be very careful how we utter reckless prayers. Poor Elijah asked to die one day in a fit of discouragement, and we only hear of him once again as a prophet.

Jonah asked in a petulant moment that he might die, and from that moment Jonah disappears from the page of history and passes into an oblivion which has upon it no ray of hope or light of recompense. The best way to be prepared to die is to be living for some high and noble purpose. The men that are ready to die are the men that are needed most to live for God and their fellow men.

10. We learn one more lesson from Jonah's life, and that is the true secret how to die, and then how to live for God and our own highest interest and blessing.

Thank God, Jonah's life lifts our thoughts to another and a nobler life, even that of the Lord Jesus Christ, who has died for us, and taught us not only how to live with Him, but also how to die with Him, and live the life that has been crucified with Christ, and is alive forevermore.

Not unwillingly, but with His whole heart did He lay down His precious life for us that in His dying we might be saved from death eternal, and then learn to die with Him, and live by Him, the life of unselfish love for God and men.

Not for His own glory did He live and die, but for us and for His Father. He died for us that we might live; yes, He died for us that we might die, and then live the crucified life and the life that is dead to self and sin.

Only through His dying can we truly die. We never can crucify ourselves, but we can be crucified with Christ, and say: "Nevertheless I live; yet not I, but Christ liveth in me: and the life which I now live in the flesh I live by the faith of the Son of God, who loved me, and gave himself for me."

Then let us learn to die, and thus let us live, and some day we shall know all the meaning of these mighty words:

> He died for me that I might die,
> He lives for me that I might live,
> Oh, death so deep! oh, life so high!
> Help me to die, help me to live.

RESURRECTED, NOT RAISED

> Resurrected with my Risen Savior,
> Seated with Him at His own right hand;
> This the glorious message Easter brings me.
> This the place in which by faith I stand.
>
> Men would bid you rise to higher levels,
> But they leave you on the human plane.
> We must have a heavenly Resurrection;
> We must die with Christ and rise again.
>
> Once there lived another man within me,
> Child of earth and slave of Satan he;
> But I nailed him to the Cross of Jesus,
> And that man is nothing now to me.

Now Another Man is living in me,
And I count His blessed life as mine;
I have died with Him to all my own life;
I have risen to all His life Divine.

Oh, it is so sweet to die with Jesus!
And by death be free from self and sin.
Oh, it is so sweet to live with Jesus!
As He lives the death-born life within.